D1389719

THE LIFE & TIMES OF CHRISTOPHER COLUMBUS

THE LIFE & TIMES OF

Christopher Columbus

BY
Timothy Moffett

This edition first published by Parragon Books

Produced by
Magpie Books Ltd
7 Kensington Church Court
London W8 4SP

Copyright © Parragon Book Service Ltd 1994

Cover picture & illustrations courtesy of: The Mary Evans
Picture Library; Christies Images.

ISBN 1 85813 917 1

A copy of the British Library Cataloguing in Publication
Data is available from the British Library.

Typeset by Hewer Text Composition Services, Edinburgh
Printed in Singapore by Printlink International Co.

Columbus's World

There are some years in history that mean something to nearly everybody. 1066 is one such year; 1789 is another; and 1492 is a third.

Before 1492, our world was small; afterwards it began to look much, much bigger. You only have to look at any map made before then to realise how little we knew about the planet we lived on – or, to put it another way, how much there was to discover.

Europe, the cradle of civilisation, visually appears more or less accurately, with the leg of Italy fully formed and the serpent's head of Scandinavia reaching down through the North Sea. But the rest of the globe is at best embryonic, at worst non-existent. Africa fizzles out somewhere around what we now know as Sudan, and the Nile is often made to run west to east across the continent, instead of south to north. Asia sometimes includes a rudimentary stump meant to represent India, but peters out thereafter. North and South America, Australasia and Antarctica are nowhere to be seen.

It is ironic, of course, that the geographers of the ancient world – so much closer in spirit to our world than to the terrified innocents of the Middle Ages – should have understood so much about the globe that would later have to be (re)discovered by the likes of Christopher Columbus. Ptolemy, for instance, knew the world was round and made a good stab at calculating its dimensions. Greek and Roman writers were aware of the existence of China and wrote about its people, its landscape and economy. But from the fifth century until the journeys of Marco Polo, the East was no more than the faintest echo in the cultural memory of the West.

Intellectually as well as geographically, the post-classical era was a time of drastically reduced horizons. Scholars, by which we mean religious scholars because there was no other type, closed their minds to the ways of empirical enquiry; indeed one early Father of the church declared that 'to investigate or wish to know the cause of things' was to go against the will of God. Knowledge that did not conform to the teachings of the Church was simply suppressed. The Apostles were commanded by Christ to go into all the world and preach to every creature – how, then, could there be unknown continents inhabited by pagans, unless the Apostles were to be accused of shirking their work? The notion that there might be an Antipodes inhabited by human beings was ridiculed by Cosmas Indicoplastes in his *Christian Topography* as 'opposed to reason and alien to our nature and condition'.

Meanwhile ordinary people dwelt in a state of perpetual oscillation between terror of the unknown and wonder at the riches it might have in store. It was popularly believed that if you sailed due west from Europe you would either drop off the edge of the world or reach a 'torrid zone' where ships dissolved in a bubbling stew. In Africa were men with the faces and tails of dogs, and serpents a mile long. Christian missionaries told tales of an oriental prince, a pious descendant of one of the Three Wise Men, who had his fabulously wealthy empire somewhere in 'the Indies'. So widespread was the belief in this mythical figure, known as Prester John, that in 1221 the Pope sent two legates to show solidarity with the prince's battle against the forces of Islam. The friars never located him.

By the beginning of the fifteenth century, however, with the Italian Renaissance in full swing and classical culture once more in the ascendant, the mists of legend and superstition began to clear and a new spirit of curiosity crept into the discourse of the time. In his *Natural Questions*, Abelard of Bath had wondered 'Why is the earth suspended in mid-air, and how is it maintained?' Marco Polo had returned from Peking with tales of the Great Khan and his untold riches, and even though he too was prone to exaggeration ('there are pearls in great quantity and so many precious stones that you only have to bend down and pick them up') the effect of his work was to open European minds to the possibilities – financial, political and missionary – of exploring the unknown. There are direct links between Polo and Columbus: we know the latter was an avid student of the Venetian's *Travels*, and Polo's account of the island of 'Cipangu' was to fascinate Columbus until his dying day.

The first fruits of the new exploratory spirit were the discoveries of the great Portuguese seamen, from Henry The Navigator and Gil

Eannes to Bartolome Diaz and Vasco da Gama. During the second half of the fifteenth century the Portuguese worked their way down the west coast of Africa, past the point known as Cape Nam – 'he who would pass Cape Nam will not return', warned a contemporary proverb – before Vasco da Gama finally rounded Cape Horn.

It was around this time that the compass, a device previously known only to the Arabs and Chinese, made its appearance on European ships. This was a moment of crucial importance in the history of our civilisation, because it meant that ships need no longer cling to the shore but could venture out into the deep ocean without losing their bearings. The compass made possible Portuguese visits to Iceland and their discovery of the Cape Verde islands, Madeira and the archipelago of the Azores, more than a thousand miles west of Lisbon.

The westernmost point of Portuguese explorations in the fifteenth century is marked by the island of Flores, discovered by Diego de Teive in 1452. Beyond that was wilderness, a great imponderable void, just as mysterious and awe-inspiring to the Renaissance mind as the vastness of outer space is to us now. It is worth considering, when we come to assess the life and work of Christopher Columbus, whether his personal victory over this great horror of the unknown wasn't one of his most remarkable achievements.

Early Years

A number of claims have been made for the birthplace of Columbus, some more far-fetched than others. Various historians have argued for Greece, England, France, Corsica and even Switzerland. One author, keen to stake his claim for Columbus's Catalan roots, suggests that his true origins lie in the 'Isla de Genova' near Tortosa in Catalonia. Another has spent years gathering scraps of 'evidence' for his theory that the discoverer of America was born on the island of Ibiza.

But history can only tolerate one authorised version of events, and that is that Christopher Columbus was born around 1450 in Genoa, to humble parents. We can be almost certain that his father was Domenico Colombo, a weaver. In his copious writings the adult Columbus scarcely mentions his background – possibly because he is ashamed of it – but admits at one point that his patrons, the King and Queen of Spain, have 'raised me up from nought'.

Fifteenth-century Genoa was a wealthy seafaring city-state whose trade links stretched from the Levant and the Black Sea in the East to the Maghreb, Portugal and Spain in the West. To a Genoese boy from a working-class household looking for a career, seamanship would have seemed a perfectly logical choice. From footnotes and jottings in Columbus's later works we can deduce that his travels as a young man, perhaps in his father's business, buying wool or selling material, took him not only all around the Mediterranean, but also to the limits of the familiar in what was known of the Atlantic: Iceland, the Azores, the west coast of Ireland, and the Gulf of Guinea in Portuguese Africa. 'From a very small age,' he wrote at the end of his life, 'I went sailing upon the sea, which very occupation inclines all who follow it to wish to learn the secrets of the world.'

If his navigational skills were acquired by practical means, Columbus's inspiration and much of his intellectual apparatus came from books. Of the works we can be certain he read, because his own copies can still be seen

Christopher Columbus

Friar Antonio de Marchena, astronomer and
advisor to Columbus

in the library of Seville Cathedral, one is Pierre d'Ailly's *Imago Mundi*, a work of great importance among the cosmographical speculations of the day. D'Ailly's influence on Columbus derives from two of his theories: that the Antipodes existed, and that most of the world's surface was covered by a single landmass uniting Europe, Asia and the Antipodes. The Atlantic was therefore the single barrier between Europe and 'the Indies', and the ocean less formidable than had previously been believed. In d'Ailly's words, 'the sea is small between the western extremity of Spain and the eastern part of India.'

The theory of a narrow Atlantic was also espoused by the Florentine cosmographer Paolo del Pozzo Toscanelli, who estimated in a letter to the King of Portugal in 1474 that between the Canaries and 'Cathay' lay

5000 nautical miles of ocean. It was a long way, but stop-offs could be made in 'Antillia', a mythical Portuguese island in the deep Atlantic, or, perhaps more conveniently, in 'Cipangu', thought to lie 1500 miles off the coast of China. Columbus approved of this view enough to copy Toscanelli's letter by hand and bind it into one of his own books, but the distance was too great for his liking. 'This world is small', he opined. Though it is a moot point whether he had formulated any clear idea of the breadth of the Atlantic by the time of his first voyage in 1492, when he came to summarise his theories later in life he estimated the size of the globe to at least 25 per cent smaller than what we know to be true.

Perhaps the most important influence on Columbus's vision, however, was Ptolemy's *Geography* – recently rehabilitated by Western scholars and an important bridging-point between classical erudition and Renaissance views of a round, rationally ordered world. Ptolemy reinforced Columbus's nascent conviction that Asia and Europe formed a continuous landmass and that between the extremities of both lay the Atlantic. All that the would-be discoverer had to do was sail across it.

If there is much about Columbus that is methodical, cool-headed and accessible to reason, there is also much that's credulous, acquisitive and unscientific. One of his favourite books was the *Travels* of Marco Polo, which he clearly relished for its tales of fabulous riches and sexual licence as much as for its information that no less than 1378 islands lay off the coast of Asia (he made a special note of this passage). In that early example of armchair travel, the journeys of Sir John Mandeville, Columbus's attention was attracted by the endless descriptions of 'spices, pearls, precious gems, cloth of gold, marble' and other marvels. It is important to recognise that the motive for Columbus's endeavours was almost as much the desire for wealth and social advancement as it was an altruistic urge to find out 'the secrets of the world'.

Almost everything about Columbus's life and achievements is a matter for controversy, from his nationality to his eventual place of burial. But it seems that at some time in the 1480s he gave up an early career as a cloth merchant and took up the trades of bookseller and cartographer. It also seems that at some point early in the decade he was married to Filipa Moniz Perestrello, a Portuguese noblewoman with whom he settled on the island of Porto Santo, off Madeira.

Gradually Columbus's plans took shape. He would strike out west with one of three aims: to discover the Antipodes; to follow Marco Polo to the treasure houses of Cipangu; or to locate a few of the Atlantic islands – probably no more than mirages – apparently glimpsed by sailors west of the Azores. We shall never know which of the three was uppermost in his mind as he conceived his great adventure, or whether indeed he gave equal weight to each.

By the close of the decade, in any case, Columbus had a selection of ends in view. Now he began to think about the means. He began, we might say, to look for sponsorship.

The first event in Columbus's life that can be dated with total certainty is his meeting with King John of Portugal in 1484. Though we don't know what was said at this meeting, the first step in his search for a patron, it is obvious from subsequent events that the King gave the thumbs-down to Columbus's plans. Joam de Barras, a somewhat unreliable chronicler writing a century after the event, imagines that the king, 'as he observed this Christovao Colon to be a big talker and more boastful in setting forth his accomplishments, and more full of fancy with his Isle Chypango, than certain of what he spoke, gave him small credit'. His proposals were considered fairly, says Barras, but were ultimately found by a committee of experts, including the Bishop of Ceuta, to be 'vain' and 'simply founded upon imagination'.

Undeterred by this initial setback, Columbus turned his attention to the court of Castile and the Catholic Kings, Ferdinand and Isabella. This was a shrewd move: preoccupied with winning back Spanish territory from the Moors, the Castilians had spent relatively little effort on Atlantic exploration, apart from their colonization of the Canary Islands. Here was a welcome chance to get one up on the Portuguese.

The seduction of the King and Queen was not to be easy or short, but Columbus knew there were certain temptations they would eventually find irresistible. Encumbered by the cost of the 1474-9 war with Portugal and the drawn-out reconquest of Granada, the Castilian economy needed a huge injection of capital; if this Genoese adventurer was correct and the treasure islands of Asia lay within a few weeks' sail from Seville, the expedition would certainly provide this. They must also have found attractive Columbus's suggestion that some of the profits of his trip would be channelled into a campaign to win back Jerusalem from the Moslems. Inspired in part by the writings of the thirteenth-century prophet Arnau de Vilanova, they themselves entertained a similar fantasy of proclaiming themselves King and Queen of Jerusalem and presiding over a world-wide Christian empire.

Basing himself in Seville, Columbus began to put down roots in high society, forging especially close links with two of the most powerful Castilian noblemen, the Very Magnificent Don Enrique de Guzmán, Duke of Medina Sidonia, and the Count of Medinaceli. The latter, who owned his

Columbus' fleet during the first voyage

Title page from the first account of Columbus' travels

own merchant fleet, must have given Columbus and his ideas some credence since he offered to provide three ships for the voyage at his own expense. Sometime in the mid-to-late 1480s Columbus came into contact with the Franciscan friars at the priory of La Rábida, in the port of Palos de la Frontera (from where his first transatlantic voyage would eventually set sail). This was an influential community which was to provide him with much moral and spiritual support in the years ahead.

Isabella of Castile and Ferdinand of Aragon, married in 1469 as monarchs of a united Spain, were a formidable couple. he was sanguine, cool, a master of diplomacy; she was ruthless, passionate, yet penetratingly intelligent. Like all monarchs and people of great fame and wealth, they had their court and circles, and it was unthinkable that a commoner like Columbus – a *foreign* commoner at that – should be admitted to their presence without a top-level introduction. Social leverage was offered by the Duke and Count, by high-ranking Genoese financiers and by business acquaintances like the treasury official Alonso de Quintanilla. The smoothest path was to be provided by Prince Don Juan, heir to the throne. Many of Don Juan's courtiers and 'staff' were associates of Columbus's, and the Prince's nurse, Juana de Torres y Ávila, and his tutor, Fray Diego Deza, both became confidantes whom Columbus exploited for their closeness to the Queen.

At Columbus's first audience in Cordoba in 1486, it was on Isabella that he made the greatest impression, while the rest of the court appears to have treated him with something close to mockery. It was her voice alone that suggested his plans shouldn't be rejected out of hand, but should be looked into by a commission of cosmographers and churchmen headed by her own confessor, Fray Hernando de Talavera.

Not every member of the Queen's commission disapproved of Columbus, but its conclusion, after several years of deliberation, was nevertheless a stern and resounding negative.

It was another disappointment, but at this stage of his career Columbus was used to them. His project now had an unstoppable momentum. At the monastery of La Rábida, where according to one tradition he'd left his young son Diego in the care of the monks, he met a sea-captain from the nearby port of Palos, Martín Alonso Pinzón, who was enthusiastic about the voyage and offered to join his team. Thanks to two friars at La Rábida, one of whom was a much respected friend of the Queen, another approach was made to the Court.

The circumstances of Columbus's successful petition have passed into the realms of romance. Granted a small allowance by the Queen to pay for decent clothes, the story goes, he got on his mule and rode to Santa Fe, where the Castilian court were awaiting the fall of Granada. Distracted by the siege, the authorities gave him the brush-off once again, and Columbus rode sadly away towards Palos. But, as she and her husband rode in triumph into Granada, the Queen remembered his plight and – perhaps in the euphoria of the moment – sent a messenger after himto disclose that his great scheme was to go ahead.

Thus, if you believe the legend, 2 January 1492 was his, and Spains, day of glory.

The First Voyage

One might have expected Columbus to be so satisfied with the outcome of his dealings with the King and Queen that he would ease up on his own demands of them once the deal was clinched. But this would be to underestimate his obstinacy, his almost pathological egoism and his deep-rooted desire for social advancement. If he were to undertake this voyage for the glory of Castile, he told Ferdinand and Isabella,

Columbus lands on San Salvador

The fort of La Navidad

the following conditions would have to be met:

1: Columbus would be made Admiral of the Seas – a hereditary title, to be handed down to his son and his son's son – and Viceroy of any new continents and islands that he might discover.

2. He would claim 10 per cent of the profits of the voyage, 'be it pearls, jewels, or any other things, that may be found, gained, bought, or exported from the countries which he is to discover'.

3. He would be given power of jurisdiction over 'all mercantile matters that may be the occasion of dispute in the countries which he is to discover'.

4. He would have the right 'to contribute the eighth part of the expenses of all ships which traffic with the new countries, and in return to earn the eighth part of the profits'.

These were extraordinarily ambitious claims. But it shows, perhaps, what high hopes the monarchs entertained of Columbus's enterprise that they were prepared to concede every one of them, apart from a slight modification to the third. They were drawn up into the Articles of Agreement and signed by all three parties, along with a letter from the King and Queen commending their new Admiral to Prester John, the Great Khan or any other Asian potentate he might come across.

The expedition left from Palos on 3 August 1492. It was a modest affair comprising three ships: the *Pinta*, captained by Martín Pinzón; the *Niña*, under his brother, Vicente Pinzón; and the ill-fated flagship *Santa María*, larger and slower than the other two, under Columbus himself. The ships carried around ninety crew in all (some twenty-five of whom were criminals given a royal pardon in return for volunteering) and provisions of biscuit, flour, salt cod and meat, dried peas, olive oil, wine and water.

Columbus planned to sail via the Canary Islands rather than the Azores, which would have brought him face to face with the rival Portuguese. He reached the port of San Sebastián de la Gomera in under a month and on 6 September, after a delay of three days caused by damage to the rudder of the *Pinta*, set off westwards on his journey into the unknown.

One can well imagine the mixture of euphoria and fear with which the sailors of the little fleet watched the peak of Mount Teide on Tenerife, the last visible point of the known world, disappear into the summer mists. It was to be a short crossing, but not always an easy one. Martín Pinzón, captain of a smaller, swifter ship than the *Santa María*, began to show signs of the wilfulness that was to be curiously common among Columbus's subordinates. At several moments there was near-mutiny as the men demanded their leader abandon his search for land and return to Spain.

There was plenty on this voyage to disturb even the most experienced seaman: from the Sargasso Sea's immense fields of mysterious yellow weed, which the crew feared might trap the ships forever in their clinging fronds, to the unexpected changeability of the compass needle, now understood as the natural result of the mobility of the North Star. The atmosphere among the crew was charged with a cocktail of emotions, among which was a strong element of religious devotion. Rudimentary services were held on board at daybreak and at sunset, and hourly throughout the night a ship's boy sang a hymn, beseeching the Virgin Mary to 'Protect us from the waterspout/And send no tempest nigh.'

There were, nevertheless, neither water-spouts nor tempests on Columbus's first crossing of the Atlantic. Side-stepping more problematic issues, he records in his captain's log that the weather was 'like April in Andalucía. There is nothing lacking save the sound of nightingales.' His choice of

the Canaries, just off the twenty-eighth
parallel, as a point of departure meant that
he was sure to have the north-east trade
winds behind him. Once his ships had set
sail from Gomera his course was simple: due
west, in a straight line, until he struck land.

Towards the middle of September, Columbus's diary begins to record sightings of
flocks of birds, whales, cloudbanks, land
crabs and other phenomena, or 'a little rain
without wind, a sure sign that land is near'.
On the 25th he had a feeling, apparently
unsubstantiated, that the ships were passing
between islands, and by the first week in
October the crew began to notice flotsam in
the water. On 11 October Columbus himself thought he saw a light on the horizon,
and as the sun went down that evening he
made the famous promise of a silken coat to

the first man to see land. Ferdinand and Isabella had also promised a life pension. At two o'clock the next morning it happened. A look-out on the *Pinta* was first to give the call of 'Tierra, tierra!', but since his Admiral said he'd sighted land the night before, the crewman in question was denied both the silken coat and the royal pension.

Where exactly was this first discovered point of the New World? Columbus gives a few clues in his log-book: it was a flat island with a lagoon in the middle and a reef around the shore, inhabited by native tribes who called it Guanahaní. (Its 'discoverer' christened it San Salvador, which may or may not have anything to do with the San Salvador of today, formerly known as Watling Island.) It was fertile, well-watered and full of fruit. But none of this information, even the native name, has enabled historians to locate it again. Having briefly emerged from the shadows of the unknown, it has slunk back into them again.

As soon as he set foot on the island, Columbus wasted no time in following up his two main concerns about it: could it possibly be Cipangu, and how much would it yield him in gold, pearls and precious stones? He soon realised that the answer to the first question was 'No'; and neither were Santa María de la Concepción, Fernandina and Isabela, the next three islands he found. But he felt he was getting nearer when he heard about the Caniba (Carib) people – clearly there was a family resemblance here to the Great Khan.

As for his longed-for gold, there was little to be found apart from the bits of primitive jewellery, made of low-grade metal, which the natives were happy to exchange for Spanish needles, scissors, mirrors, beads and other cheap Western baubles. They seemed to have no conception of the value of things or property, he noted, but 'will give all they possess for anything that is given to them, exchanging things even for bits of broken crockery or broken glass cups'.

The next island he visited, 'Colba' (Cuba), was at first another candidate for Cipangu and then, when Columbus realised it had none of the gold-covered rooftops or sumptuous gardens of Marco Polo's description, had to be the coast of Cathay itself. He was sufficiently convinced of being within striking distance of the Great Khan to send inland a 'fact-finding mission', including a Hebrew-speaking interpreter, to try to find his court and the city of Quinsay (Chankow). It was a shame for Columbus that not only had the Great Khan been dead for more than two centuries, but the coast of Cathay, the real Asia, lay a good 9000 miles further west.

In Hispaniola (Haiti), the final discovery of his first voyage, Columbus at last found a tolerable quantity of gold and, though this was not Cipangu any more than Cuba had been, he was pleased to find a native civilisation more sophisticated and advanced than any he had yet encountered. In a place like this, he felt, the Castilian empire could really take root. The natives were friendly, credulous and timid, he wrote to Ferdinand and Isabella after a meeting with the Arawak chief, Guacanagarí: 'All the islands are so utterly at your Highnesses' command that it only remains to establish a Spanish pre-

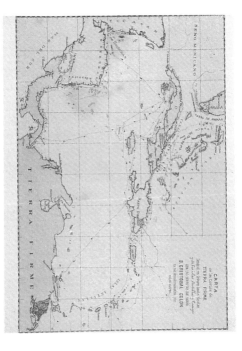

Map showing Columbus' travels in the Caribbean

Columbus meets the inhabitants of San Salvador

sence and order them to perform your will. For I could traverse all these islands in arms without meeting opposition . . . so that they are yours to command and make them work, sow seed and do whatever else is necessary and build a town and teach them to wear clothes and adopt our customs.'

The colonizing of Hispaniola was in one sense inevitable. On Christmas Eve the *Santa María* ran aground on a coral reef and the crew were forced to abandon ship. There was now no way all the men could return to Spain. Those who wished to stay would establish a garrison at Puerto de la Navidad (Port Christmas) and co-operate with Guacanagarí and his people, whom Columbus fatally misjudged as peace-loving and amenable.

As he sailed away towards Spain on 16 January 1493, leaving a little fort built mostly from the wood of his own wrecked ship, staffed by two officers in charge of thirty-six colonists, Columbus may have allowed himself a smile of satisfaction. Apart from the loss of his flagship, which he now chose to interpret as divine providence, the only serious mishap of the expedition had been the behaviour of Martín Pinzón, who had gone on a gold-hunt while his Admiral was busy building Puerto de la Navidad. He would be able to present his patrons with some amusing gifts: hammocks, canoes, a pineapple, spices, some leaves of a pungent herb which was 'highly esteemed among the Indians' (tobacco), and an amount of gold which was both impressive in itself and promised far greater riches to come.

The journey home, however, brought him nearer to total disaster than he had been at any moment in his extremely chequered career. It also brought him closer to God. At first the *Pinta* and the *Niña* were carried east by a strong following wind. Then suddenly, on 12 February, they were caught in a storm that separated the two ships and stripped both of their masts. At the height of the storm, Columbus tried to console himself in his anguish with the thought that 'our Lord would not allow such an enterprise to remain unfinished, which was so much for the exaltation of His Church and which I had brought to pass with so much travail in the face of so much hostility', and later he seems to have gone through the first of a life long series of increasingly intense mystical experiences: a heavenly voice whispering words of comfort.

Following a brief and unpleasant interlude in the Azores, when the entire crew of the *Niña* was thrown into jail, Columbus arrived in Lisbon to a not exactly warm welcome from King John, who had refused his first overtures. Columbus made it back to a triumphant reception in Castile in early April 1493 – before the *Pinta* and Martín Pinzón, who eventually arrived at Bayona on the north-west coast of Spain but died of exhaustion soon after landing.

Columbus had not in fact achieved the agreed aim of his voyage, which was to discover the western route to Asia. Nonetheless, his patrons seemed to be happy. 'It seems that everything which from the first you said could be achieved', they wrote to him a year after his return, 'has turned out for the most part to be true; as if you had seen it before you spoke of it.' He was acclaimed

Columbus' home on Haiti

Columbus' brother Giacomo

equally by the intellectual elite of Castile and by the unlettered masses. The cartographer Jaume Ferrer compared his adventures in the West to those of Saint Thomas in the East. People thronged the streets in every town as he rode past with his full *équipage* of tribesmen in their outlandish costumes, carrying spears. When he finally reached the royal palace in Seville he was addressed by Ferdinand and Isabella with the promised title of 'Don Cristobal, our Admiral of the Ocean Sea and Viceroy and Governor of the Islands which have been discovered in the Indies'.

Bartolomé de las Casas, the man whose account of the first Spanish colonies paints such a bleak picture of incompetence and brutality, describes Columbus's presentation of his own successes to his patrons:

When he had given wise account of all the graces God had given him during the voyage, and of the grandeur and felicity of the lands discovered, when he had displayed the pieces of carved gold and the specimens of gold, some in large nuggets and some in fine grains, and avowed that these lands produced such in infinite quantities; when he had described the innocence and docility of these people and their readiness to receive our Holy Faith . . . then the Sovereigns rose and kneeled, their eyes full of tears, and the choir of the royal chapel chanted the *Te Deum*.

The Second and Third Voyages

It was now a matter of urgency that Columbus undertake a second voyage to consolidate the progress made on the first. This time the expedition was a larger and more grandiose affair of seventeen ships (including the *Niña*, captained by Columbus himself) and 1300 men including colonists, troops and a squad of Franciscan friars for the conversion of the Arawaks of Hispaniola.

After a minor detour in which Dominica,

Puerto Rico and Guadelupe were added to the growing list of Castilian dominions, the fleet arrived at the embryonic colony of Puerto de la Navidad, where it was clear that something had gone terribly wrong. The men holding the garrison had all been killed, and the fort was a charred ruin. It seemed the Arawaks were not quite as innocent and docile as Columbus had fancied.

Chief Guacanagarí had his own explanation for the turn of events. The lust and greed of those Spaniards who had stayed behind had become intolerable, and when they had tried to steal gold from a neighbouring chief they had paid with their lives. Guacanagarí said he had actually tried to protect them, but to no avail.

Columbus chose to give the natives the benefit of the doubt; but the massacre at Navidad was an ominous start to his career as a colonial governor.

Columbus's next project, a coastal township which he called Isabela and founded in January 1494, wasn't much more of a success. The men were ill from the strange diet, the European livestock languished or died, and the stock of grain was ground into flour instead of planted.

Meanwhile there were rumours of gold in a region of the interior called, no doubt tantalisingly for Columbus, 'Cibao'. He dispatched Captain Alonso de Hojeda to investigate. When Hojeda came back with tales of 'gold in so many places that no one dared to guess the number', Columbus decided to mount a full-scale expedition. It was an egregious disappointment. There were a few bits of jewellery and other artefacts given them by the natives of Cibao, but nothing like the fabulous riches they had been led to expect.

Frustrated by the non-availability of gold and worried by the escalating level of violence between settlers and natives, Columbus decided to leave Isabela to its own devices, reconnoitre Jamaica and revisit Cuba, which he wanted to prove beyond all doubt was a part of the Asian mainland. More than one historian has conjectured that the treacherous sailing between these islands and the stress and sleeplessness it caused Columbus may have brought him to the brink of madness. Certainly some explanation is required for his strange behaviour. Descriptions of a man dressed in white

The return of Columbus

Columbus' ship the *Santa Maria*

made Columbus think again about Prester
John – 'a saintly king of great estate who held
infinite provinces and wore a white tunic' –
and he found re-echoes of Marco Polo in local
place-names like Mangon ('Mangi' was Polo's
name for South China). He began to talk in
earnest about his plan to sail around the world
via the Ganges, Jerusalem and Jaffa, liberating
the Holy Sepulchre on the way. Most unac-
countably of all, he forced every member of his
crew to swear on oath that Cuba was a
continent, not an island. If any man was heard
to deny this 'fact' in future, he would be fined
10,000 *maravedis* and his tongue would be cut
out. It was the brutality of a man who had lost
his reason.

When he got back to Hispaniola there was
more bad news. Fray Boil, a missionary, had
returned to Castile to denounce Columbus's

poor government of the colony and to complain about the enslavement of Indians. (The Church disapproved of slavery if the victims of it could be considered as potential Christians.) The King and Queen were so alarmed by these reports that in late 1495 they commissioned a judicial inquiry into Columbus's progress as governor of their new colony.

Meanwhile the town of Isabela was practically under a state of siege from native attacks. The response of Columbus and his deputies, his brother Bartolomé and Alonso de Hojeda, was to crush the rebellion by whatever means possible. Caonabo, the chief thought to have masterminded the Navidad massacre, was taken prisoner. The islanders were taxed and put to work. According to Bartolomé de las Casas, two-thirds of the indigenous population of Hispaniola was wiped out in a series of bloody battles in the winter and spring of 1494–5.

Columbus was an explorer, not an administrator. Proof of this, if proof were needed, was given by his third voyage. It was undertaken in 1498, after Ferdinand and Isabella had had plenty of time to assuage their doubts about his achievements thus far. Its main aim was a major exploration of the uncharted Atlantic.

This time Columbus would aim much further south, doubtless bearing in mind the notion, fashionable among cosmographers, that the closer one went to the Equator the more fertile and rich (i.e. in gold) the land became.

It was high summer. Taking as his stop-off point the wild and woolly Cape Verde islands, Columbus sailed straight into the doldrums and stayed there for a week, roasting under a merciless sun that left the ships without water or food. Emerging from this hell he stumbled on Trinidad, named after the three hills that were his first sight of the island, and then made what is probably the most significant discovery of his life. Across the water from Trinidad was another land he called Tierra de Grácia. While perusing the coast, he stumbled upon on immense estuary discharging a flood of sweet water. It dawned on him that if this was a river it must have flowed an enormous distance – too much to be accommodated by any island. Either this was the original site of Paradise (there are four mouths of the Orinoco, just as there were four great rivers flowing from the Garden of Eden) or this was the real thing: a previously unknown continent. For once he seems to have abandoned his obsession with Asia, and recognised this new land as having no connection with anything mentioned by Marco Polo. On 13 August he wrote in his journal, 'I believe this is a very large continent which until now has remained unknown', and promised his long-suffering patrons 'Your Highnesses will gain these lands, which are another world.' It is often said glibly that Columbus discovered America. This is true, but only in so far as it derives from this moment, when he came across a landmass which he realised was distinct and separate from all others yet visited by Europeans.

From Venezuela he moved on reluctantly to Hispaniola, where his brother Bartolomé Colón, now *adelantado* (commander) of the island and violently unpopular among the

Spaniards, had set up the new town of Santo Domingo and was struggling to bring the Indian population under control. Worst of all, his Chief Justice and former friend, Francisco Roldán, had led an insurrection against the island's Genoese oligarchy. The rebels' main demand was not money or land, but a free passage home to Castile. In his biography of his father, Columbus's son Fernando says that fifty returned settlers turned up at the court of the Catholic Kings to protest at the low pay they had received in their service to the State. On seeing Fernando, who was one of Isabella's pages, they shouted: 'Look at the son of the Admiral of Mosquitoland, of that man who has discovered the lands of deceit and disappointment, a place of sepulchre and wretchedness to Spanish *hidalgos*!'

Columbus welcomed back by Ferdinand and Isabella

Columbus' second wife Beatriz

The colony had become a miserable place to be – especially if you happened to have been born there. A particularly unjust form of slavery known as the *encomienda* – whereby groups of Indians were apportioned to the colonists, to be used in whatever ways they saw fit – had been introduced (and sanctioned by Columbus) to make up for the meagre share-out of gold. The natives were as defenceless against European diseases, now rife on Hispaniola, as they were against European weapons.

In September 1499 there was a new and dangerous challenge to Columbus's authority in the shape of Alonso de Hojeda, who had mounted his own expedition from Andalucía and turned up on Hispaniola, rousing the natives to further acts of insurrection not only against Columbus himself, but also against the rebel chief Roldán. The chaos worsened the following year, when a further rebellion against both Columbus and Roldán resulted in its leader, Adrián de Muxica, being condemned to death. According to one account, he was thrown from a church tower, while six of his associates were hung in the main square of Santo Domingo.

The King and Queen, meanwhile, had lost their patience again. It was time to replace their Viceroy with someone who could restore order. Indeed, Columbus practically recognised as much himself. But he cannot have liked the manner in which Francisco de Bobadilla went about his task. Columbus and his brothers were clapped in irons, imprisoned for two months and finally sent back to Spain in disgrace. Outraged and humi-

liated by his treatment, Columbus refused to
remove his shackles when the opportunity
came but shuffled in, still wearing them, to
see the Queen.

Columbus was slipping into mental derange-
ment. On the third voyage, he had regularly
heard his 'celestial voice'. Now his thoughts
turned to the favourite fantasy of his later life:
the recapture of Jerusalem for Castile. He
would never again be allowed to assume a
position of power, but Ferdinand and Isabella hadn't entirely rejected his suit. In 1500
he produced for them a bizarre document
entitled 'The Reason I have for Believing in
the Restoration of the Holy House to the
Holy Church Militant', which presents his
discoveries as divinely inspired and alludes to
the Old Testament prophets in support of his
'crusade'. According to his interpretation of

St Augustine, moreover, there were only 155 years to go until the end of the world. There was therefore no time to lose.

A further stimulus to his fevered brain was given by news of Vasco da Gama's successful voyage to India and the spectacular publicity-stunt laid on by the Portuguese at the court of the Zamorin of Calicut. This, in particular, must have been a bitter blow to his ego, for it seemed India was yielding up the gold, gems, and spices that had been so conspicuously lacking in the Spanish Indies.

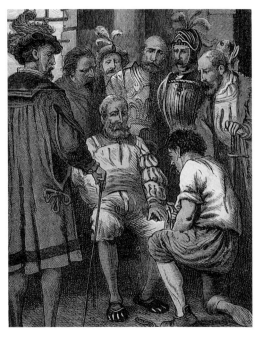

Columbus put in chains

Tiled fountain showing portrait of
Christopher Columbus

The Final Voyage

Columbus was, as he intimated to a friend in May 1501, 'in disgrace, low in the favour of (the) monarchs, and with little money'. But by the beginning of 1502, after a year of writing letters to the Pope, re-establishing his contacts with the Genoese community in Castile and campaigning hard to win back the trust of Ferdinand and Isabella, his luck began to turn. A year later, he was ready to embark once more.

The aims of this, his final and least successful voyage, were vague even by his own standards. Released from his arduous responsibilities as Viceroy, he was free to resume the exploration of 'Paria' – the coast of Central and South America, as they would now be known – which had got off to such a promising start on his third voyage. He would sail among the islands of the Caribbean, find a passage through Paria, and stop off among the gold mines of Asia *en route* to Jerusalem and home. It was even seriously considered that he might meet up with Vasco da Gama, who was about to undertake his second trip to India.

He was discouraged from setting foot on Hispaniola by the King; but Santo Domingo would be a natural watering-place after the transatlantic crossing. As he came close to the

island with his four small ships a terrible
storm was brewing. He asked for permission
to use the harbour but was refused, and took
refuge in a sheltered bay. By what must have
seemed to Columbus like natural justice, a
fleet carrying his old adversaries Francisco
Roldán and Francisco de Bobadilla was just
leaving Santo Domingo. It was utterly de-
stroyed by the storm and 500 lives were lost.

Limping away westwards with his tattered
ships, he made land on the coast of Honduras
and, believing it to be 'Paria', turned east in
search of a strait through which he would pass
to reach India. If he had only turned west, he
would shortly have come upon the untold
riches of the Maya empire and his fortunes
would have taken a decisive turn for the better.
As it was, all that remained was misery, hard-
ship and sheer bad luck. The crew were sick,

and in September 1502 the Admiral himself was 'close to death'. The weather was atrocious. 'No eyes ever saw a sea so high and ugly and foaming', he wrote. '. . . There I remained, on that sea of blood that boiled like a cauldron on a huge fire. So fearful a sky was never seen.' Things looked up a little when, in early 1503, they reached the gold-rich river and friendly Indians of Veragua. But the natives turned nasty, the gold proved hard to get at, and the ships became riddled with termites and practically unseaworthy.

In his desperation, Columbus turned north and made once more for Hispaniola. His 'celestial voice' had turned from a whisper to a scream of bitter self-justification, ranting about God-given achievements and biblical sufferings. He made it as far as St Ann's Bay on Jamaica, where the ships gave out, and survived for a year on rat-meat and cassava bread until, following a daring five-day canoe journey by Diego Mendez de Salcedo, a rescue vessel finally arrived from Santo Domingo in June 1504.

By the end of the same year, the Very Magnificent Lord Don Cristobal Colon, Grand Admiral of the Ocean Sea, was back in Castile, a broken man. Queen Isabella, who for the last twenty years had been one of the mainstays of Columbus's life, died not long after his return from the Indies. He was in poor health, and had to be carried from place to place on a stretcher. 'This trouble of mine is so bad, and the cold aggravates it so, that I shall be unlikely to avoid ending up in some inn', he wrote, planning a trip from Seville to see the King in Segovia.

The last eighteen months of Columbus's life were principally spent trying to extract from the royal coffers the money he felt had been promised to him and his descendants in the 1492 agreements. In this, as in so many other goals of his later life, he was to be frustrated. He died in May 1506 and was buried first in Valladolid, then in the family mausoleum in Seville, then in the Cathedral of Santo Domingo, and finally – if you believe those much-travelled bones are genuinely his – under a monument in Seville Cathedral.

There can be few men or women whose achievements are as well known as Columbus's, yet whose successes are so interwoven with disaster. Judged on his own terms and by his own goals, his life could be described as a failure. He neither succeeded in discovering the western route to Asia, nor reached the fabled shores of Cathay; he neither found Cipangu, nor met the Great Khan or Prester John. The fabulous riches he promised would result from his explorations were never forthcoming. His career as a governor was catastrophic – though his brutal and repressive successors could hardly be said to have improved on his record.

Against this bleak panorama, the positive aspects of a fascinating and complex man can be examined in their true light. He was the first Westerner to discover a direct route across the Atlantic; that much is certain. Though he later went back on his decision, he was aware at a certain point that he had come upon a huge continent lying to the south and west of the Caribbean. In the sense that he went from Europe to an unknown land which he correctly recognised for what it was, he can therefore be said to have discovered the continent of America – though it was left to others to reap its rewards.

In many ways Columbus was a product of his time. And yet, in his curiosity, his restlessness, and his brittle, mad courage, he appears to us now as one of the first, flawed geniuses of our modern world.

CHRONOLOGY

1450

Christopher Columbus is born into a weaver's family in Genoa.

1480

Having become a cartographer, Columbus marries Filipa Moniz Perestrello and moves to an island off Madeira. He hatches plans to discover a western route to Asia.

1484

Columbus presents his plans to King John of Portugal and is turned down.

1486

Columbus has his first audience with Ferdinand and Isabella.

1492

Ferdinand and Isabella finally approve Columbus's plans and on 3 August he sets sail across the Atlantic. Land is sighted on 11 October and

Columbus sets foot on the Caribbean islands. A colony is formed on Haiti, with a fort built from the wreck of the *Santa Maria*.

1493

Columbus sets sail for Spain and arrives at Court in April. Ferdinand and Isabella confer upon him the title of Don Cristobal.

Columbus sets out on a second voyage at the end of the year. He finds the fort on Haiti in ruins, and all the colonists killed. He makes peace with the Arawak indians and resumes colonisation.

1494

Troubles between settlers and natives grow as Columbus becomes more desperate for proof that he is close to Asia.

1495

News of the troubles on the islands reaches Spain and Ferdinand and Isabella commission a judicial inquiry into Columbus's progress as governor.

1498

On a third voyage, Columbus heads further south

and reaches the shores of Venezuela. The great river mouth persuades him that he has at last landed on a continent.

The settlers on Haiti rebel against Columbus and his brother.

1499

Rebellion grows. Ferdinand and Isabella decide to replace Columbus as Viceroy. He is brought back to Spain in chains.

1502

Back in favour with Ferdinand and Isabella, Columbus reaches Central America on his final voyage.

1503

Columbus and his crew are shipwrecked for a year on Jamaica.

1504

Columbus returns to Spain in disgrace and poor health.

1506

Columbus dies in May.

LIFE AND TIMES

Julius Caesar
Hitler
Monet
Van Gogh
Beethoven
Mozart
Mother Teresa
Florence Nightingale
Anne Frank
Napoleon

LIFE AND TIMES

JFK
Martin Luther King
Marco Polo
Christopher Columbus
Stalin
William Shakespeare
Oscar Wilde
Castro
Gandhi
Einstein

FURTHER MINI SERIES INCLUDE

ILLUSTRATED POETS

Robert Burns
Shakespeare
Oscar Wilde
Emily Dickinson
Christina Rossetti
Shakespeare's Love Sonnets

FURTHER MINI SERIES
INCLUDE

HEROES OF THE WILD WEST

General Custer
Butch Cassidy and the Sundance Kid
Billy the Kid
Annie Oakley
Buffalo Bill
Geronimo
Wyatt Earp
Doc Holliday
Sitting Bull
Jesse James

THEY DIED TOO YOUNG

Malcolm X
Kurt Cobain
River Phoenix
John Lennon
Glenn Miller
Isadora Duncan
Rudolph Valentino
Freddie Mercury
Bob Marley